Editorial Project Manager
Lorin E. Klistoff, M.A.

Managing Editors
Karen J. Goldfluss, M.S. Ed.
Ina Massler Levin, M.A.

Illustrator
Blanca Apodaca

Cover Artist
Marilyn Goldberg

Art Coordinator
Renée Christine Yates

Art Manager
Kevin Barnes

Contributing Author
Kathleen "Casey" Petersen

Imaging
James Edward Grace
Craig Gunnell

Publisher
Mary D. Smith, M.S. Ed.

Phonics POETRY

Grades K-2

- emphasizes over 30 sounds
- increases reading fluency
- builds decoding skills

The Circus

Phil, the Photographer

Choo-Choo Train

Author

Barbara Paape

Teacher Created Resources, Inc.
6421 Industry Way
Westminster, CA 92683
www.teachercreated.com

ISBN: 978-1-4206-3521-8

©*2006 Teacher Created Resources, Inc.*
Reprinted, 2012
Made in U.S.A.

Table of Contents

Introduction

Welcome! Young children can become poetry readers and yes, even poetry lovers! Each poem in *Phonics Poetry* is especially written with beginning and developing readers in mind. The poems are comprised of over 30 different sounds that beginning readers need to learn. The poems make the perfect introduction to the world of poetry for students and teachers alike.

Why write a book of phonics poems? The poems are an easy way to introduce, practice, and review important sounds in our language. Phonological awareness, or the awareness of sounds in words, is a powerful predictor of success in both reading and writing skills. Also, research has shown the usefulness of children learning different phonics sounds or "chunks." From over 30 phonics sounds, children can build many beginning words. The poems will increase a child's decoding skills and reading fluency. The simplicity of the poems and the repetitiveness of each of the sounds make it easy for students to learn to read the poems and remember the sounds.

While the poems in this book are meant to be read and enjoyed, don't stop there! Use the activities and suggestions on the following pages to bring poetry into other areas of the curriculum, like math, science, social studies, and physical education. They can be used with more than one title, more than one time. Many activities also provide opportunities to address the different levels of achievement that inevitably exist in a classroom each year. Reading these poems will leave students wanting more, so encourage new readers by finding other collections that fit the bill. Writing poetry is also a natural extension to the reading. Get students started with poetry blanks where a skeleton of a poem is in place but blank spaces exist for individual ideas. Move on from there to free verse or name poems so a child's personality can truly shine through.

Most important of all, when using this book, have fun! Developing a true enjoyment of words at an early age will lead to a lifelong love of books.

Suggestions

The following pages are suggested activities to use with the poems in this book.

❖ Hands Up

Have students close their eyes, and listen for the special sound featured in the poem. Tell them to raise their hands when they hear the sound.

❖ Scavenger Sound Hunt

Introduce the sound to students. Tell them that the poem will have several words that include the sound. Read the poem. Have your students use multi-colored highlighters to locate the specific sound. The children will enjoy using these "special" markers, and you will be able to check their progress at a glance. Then have your students read the poem to you. Next, have them take the poem home to read to their parents. The students will bring back their poems to school the next day and place them in files with their names. Have the poems ready for other activities, such as "Create Poetry Books."

❖ Marker Switch

Have students write words from the poem that contain the phonics sound on individual white boards. They can each write the sound with one color, then the rest of the word in a different color.

❖ Create Poetry Books

Feature the phonics sound from a poem each week. Begin on Monday and practice reading the poem with your students everyday. Include some of the activities from these pages during the course of the week. By Friday, each child will be comfortable with the poem and able to read it to a friend. They can then each cut out the poem, glue it into a book of blank pages, and illustrate it. By the end of the semester or year, they will each have a book of poems to take home that they can proudly read to their families.

❖ Grab Your Partner

Reproduce an appropriate poem from the book. Have each student practice it with a pre-selected partner for several days or longer. Ask the team to illustrate the poem and read it to the class. Each week another pair of students can be in the spotlight.

❖ Stick To It!

Write the poem on a large piece of chart paper and leave sticky notes nearby. Ask each child to write his or her name on a note and cover up a word he or she knows. Bring the group together and have each student uncover his or her word and "teach" it to the class. A variation on this activity is to have children cover up an unknown word and as you uncover it, say the word so everyone can benefit.

Suggestions *(cont.)*

❖ Play Spotlight

Turn off the lights in your room and give a student a flashlight. Have him or her turn on the flashlight and "spotlight" a particular word or sound. This is a great activity for all levels of readers because you can choose the word according to each child's ability.

❖ Read the Walls

Write poems on chart paper and post them around your room. Supply students with colorful pointers so they can practice reading them on their own. When introducing this activity it is important to model your expectations for pointer use so that they are used safely.

❖ Calling All Readers

Assign each child a different line of a poem you have written on chart paper and give him or her time to practice reading it. Once everyone is comfortable with his or her part, you can have a community read. (A community read is one where everyone participates by reading aloud the specific line of the poem he or she has practiced. Everyone has a chance to read and feels successful in doing so.)

❖ Pointers, Please

Throughout the course of the year, give each student an opportunity to come to the front of the class and point to the words with a pointer while the rest of the class reads the poem aloud.

❖ Transparent Poems

Make transparencies of poems. Have children come up to the overhead projector and find different letters, sounds, words, rhymes, patterns, etc. Your students will enjoy using this very grown-up machine.

❖ Pocketful of Poems

Write each line of a poem on a sentence strip. Have the children work together to place the poem in the correct order in a pocket chart. Read it as a group to check for accuracy. This can also be done on a smaller basis by cutting up copies of the poem and placing the strips into an envelope. Students can put it back in order as a center activity and ask a friend to check it.

❖ Wait Your Turn, Please

Post a poem on the board, overhead, or easel and have girls and boys alternate reading lines. Read it again and switch the order of readers.

Suggestions *(cont.)*

✣ Go Van Gogh

This activity will last almost the whole year. Each week, ask one child to illustrate the poem on which you are working. Keep the pages and create a class book of student-illustrated poetry that can be showcased at an end-of-the-year-literacy night.

✣ Vacation or "School Break" Reading

Send home several poems to read at Thanksgiving, winter break, spring break, etc. Young or remedial students often lose reading skills during vacations. Books are expensive and easy to lose (especially on trips or when visiting relatives). Send poems, instead. Grandparents and other relatvies enjoy listening to these poems.

✣ Guesses, Please

A great way to strengthen students' estimation skills is to have them guess how many of a certain thing there are in a poem. For example, students can guess how many consonants, vowels, sounds, words, or letters a poem contains. Estimates can be put into a jar during the course of the week and the answer can be decided on Friday, as a class.

✣ Graph It!

Another enjoyable tie between math and literacy can be made by having students graph the number of times a sound, sight words, vowels, consonants, individual letters of the alphabet, etc., there are in a poem. Groups of students can be responsible for counting different things and entering the information onto a giant class graph. Questions from you will give children practice with data interpretation. This activity can be tailored to specific needs or to review curriculum pieces already taught.

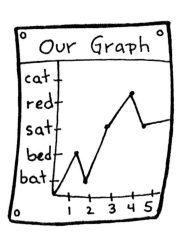

✣ Units Unite

Some of the poems can be incorporated into a unit of study. This book contains pieces about insects, transportation, feelings, friendship, night, the New Year, and much more. Poems offer a plausible link between literacy and science or social studies topics.

✣ Speech, Speech

Have each child choose a poem with which he or she is comfortable. After sufficient practice, he or she can dramatically read it in front of the class. This offers an excellent opportunity for reading with expression and with an audience in mind.

Suggestions *(cont.)*

❖ **Word Frames**

Purchase a small, inexpensive picture frame (or borrow one from home). Give it to a child during whole- or small-group time and ask him or her to come up to the chart and frame a particular word or sound. You can challenge your strong readers and target areas of difficulty for your beginning readers depending upon which word you ask him or her to frame.

❖ **Start Your Stories, Please**

Use the titles of the poems as inspirational writing prompts. Your students can write about their own grown-up wishes or recount trips they have taken—the possibilities go on and on.

❖ **Authors—On Your Marks**

Some of the poems lend themselves to being re-written. An easy way to get your students into writing poetry is to use poetry blanks. Retype a poem, leaving occasional blank spaces. (Be sure to keep the rhythm of the poem.) Let the children fill in their own ideas in each blank. As they get better at this, the blank spaces can be positioned in more challenging ways.

❖ **Lights, Camera, Action!**

Many of the poems open up the possibility for companion actions. You may find that as you read a poem aloud for the second or third time, your students invent actions to go along with the words. If not, brainstorm a set of actions that would be appropriate for the poem and practice them. You can do a "final performance" for a neighboring class, or another faculty member in the school, once your children are comfortable with their parts.

❖ **Fluency For All**

For this activity, you will be in charge of the pointer and the children will read the poem aloud as you point. Tell them that they must keep pace with the pointer at all times. Move the pointer at an appropriate pace for your students. If you pause, so must they. If you speed up, they must as well. Your students will find it amusing if you slow down or speed up considerably during this activity.

❖ **Technology, Too**

Using a painting or drawing program, have your children illustrate the week's poem on a computer. If you transfer the poem to chart paper and display it in your room, the illustrations done by the children can make a border around it. It will be a wonderful addition to your room or hallway that will make your technology coordinator proud.

Suggestions *(cont.)*

❖ Books, Books, Books

Make a poem into a book by typing each line or phrase on its own page. Staple or bind the pages together in the correct order and let each child illustrate his or her own. Or have groups of children work on pages together to make a class big book that everyone can read.

❖ ABC

Have your students highlight a pre-determined list of words in a poem. Then ask them to write the words in alphabetical order beneath it. Start with just a few words at a time. Then increase the difficulty by adding more words and words that begin with the same letter.

❖ Sticky-Note Cover-Up

This activity allows for a terrific amount of individualized instruction. You will need to reproduce the poem you want to use onto a piece of chart paper before starting. Give each child a small sticky note. Once each child has a note, call him or her up to the chart and ask him or her to cover up a specific word. For your shy or less able students, initially choose words you are certain they will know. As they become more comfortable with the group and the process, increase the difficulty of the words you give. For your more proficient readers, select words that only appear once or that do not follow phonemic rules. They will enjoy the challenge.

❖ Word Ladders

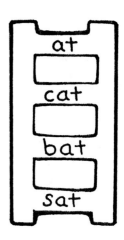

You'll need a reproducible pattern of a ladder for this activity. A hand-drawn one will work just as well as a pre-made picture. Write a key word from the poem you are using on the top rung of the ladder and make enough copies for each student in your room to have his or her own. In each of the rungs of the ladder, ask your students to write words that rhyme with the word at the top of the ladder. As your children gain confidence, the ladders can get longer.

❖ Handful of Letters

Have your students trace their hands on blank pieces of paper. Provide each student with a word to write in the palm of the traced hand. Their job is to each write one rhyming word in each of the fingers. This activity is good for challenging and reviewing, depending on your needs.

❖ Book Hunt

Read the poem and then have students look for the featured sound in other story books.

Student Book Cover

The Space Race

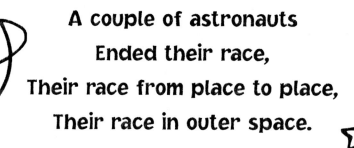

A couple of astronauts
Had a race in space,
They raced from place to place,
They raced in outer space.

A couple of astronauts
Ended their race,
Their race from place to place,
Their race in outer space.

One astronaut could not race
At such a high speed pace,
And one was a racing ace,
She has a grin upon her face!

Mr. Hall

That's my coach; that's Mr. Hall.
See him standing by the wall?

Even though I'm very small,
He says that I can bat the ball.

He has seen me playing ball;
He will coach me through it all.

I'll play ball for Mr. Hall;
He is great and very tall!

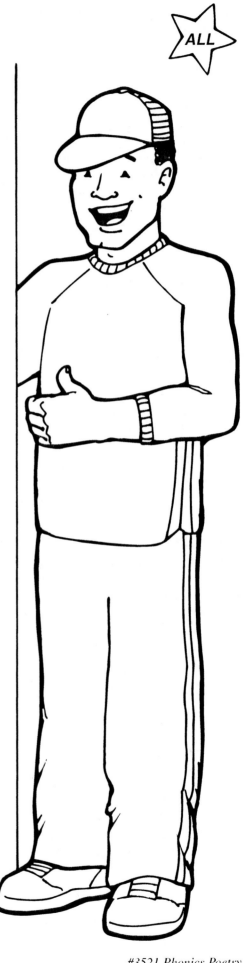

#3521 Phonics Poetry

No Ball

While waiting for my friend to call,
My friend who's fun and tall,

I waited in the long, dark hall,
The hall beside the mall.

He said we'd meet beside the wall,
The wall inside the hall,

And in the field beside the mall,
We'd kick and throw the ball.

I heard him coming down the hall,
The hall beside the mall,

I heard him trip; I heard him fall,
Oh no, we can't play ball!

4th of July

All the people sang,
And all the bells rang.
And the fire trucks went,
Clang, clang, clang!

But what I liked best,
More than all the rest . . .

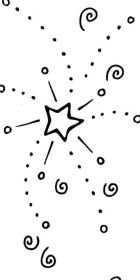

Not when people sang,
Not when bells rang,
But when the fireworks
Went "Bang, Bang, Bang!"

Cash in the Bank

If I had a lot of cash,
I'd do something rather rash.

I'd dump it all into a tank,
And then I'd drive it to the bank!

I'd be careful, as I'd dash,
For I would not want to crash.

There I'd meet the teller, Frank,
He would let me in the bank.

Then he'd say, 'cause he's a crank,
"That was quite a silly prank!"

14

The Car

I'd like to have a bright, red car,
And in my car, I'd go far!

I like to think I'd go so far
That I would find a farm afar!

Farms with bright, red barns are
Just as nice as my red car.

Then I'd like to go so far
That I could touch a shining star!

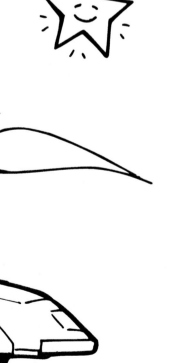

My Puppy's Paw

One day when we were at the park,
I saw my puppy hurt his paw!

I ran to where I'd heard him bark,
I saw him bawl; I dropped my jaw!

I called out for some help with him,
Some kids upon the see-saw saw!

They ran across the grassy field
To help my puppy with his paw!

Today

Today, I say
Is a day for play!

Not a hurry-up and
Go-to-school day!

It's a stay-at-home and
Let's-play day!

It's a sunshiny
Happy play day,

Not a gloomy, gray,
No-time-to-play day.

It's a wonderful, beautiful day!
It's . . . Saturday!

The Circus

A creepy, crawly circus
Is coming to my town
With fleas who cycle madly
In circles 'round and 'round.

The center ring is crazy,
Caterpillars on cars
And corny, yellow lizards
Are crawling on the bars!

Choo-Choo Train

Choo-choo, choo-choo train,
Coming down the track,
Choo-choo, choo-choo train,
From Chico town and back!

It's bringing cherries, sweet,
It's bringing chocolate, too,
It's bringing cheese for Pete,
It's bringing chips for you!

Choo-choo, choo-choo train,
Chugging through the town.
Choo-choo, choo-choo train,
It chimes its lovely sound.

A Good New Year

The bells I hear
This New Year,
I gather 'round
My friends, so dear.

Noisy clappers
Near my ear,
Make me jump
And hide with fear!

I will smile
And wipe my tear
And wish you all
A good New Year!

Going Down the Street

What did I see
Going down the street?
A large monster I saw
With his one-hundred feet!

What did I see
Going down the street?
A bumble bee I saw
Next to a parakeet!

Who did I see
Going down the street?
Mr. Green, I saw
With daughter, Kimberlee!

What did I see
Going down the street?
A chickadee, I saw
And a big chimpanzee!

Water

A raindrop is so small,
There isn't much that's smaller,

But put a lot together,
And a puddle is much bigger.

A puddle might be big,
But a stream is even bigger.

A stream is not the biggest,
For a pond, you see, is bigger.

A pond is pretty big,
But a river is much bigger.

A river might be huge,
But a lake can be much bigger.

A lake is very big,
But the ocean is the biggest!

Look at how these all
Come from raindrops small!

The Test

In school today
We had a test,

About the topic
Of the West.

For some it was
A tough contest.

For me it was
A peaceful rest,

About the topic
Of the West.

I have to say,
I am a pest.

For on this topic,
I am the best!

I love to learn
About the West!

I Wish I Knew

I wish I knew
How those flowers grew.

I wish I knew
How that butterfly flew.

I wish I knew
What made that dew.

So many things,
I wish I knew.

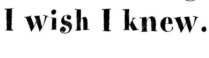

The Gentle Giant

The gentle giant
Lived all alone
In a cave full of gems—
How brightly they shone!

Geraniums bloomed
Outside the cave door;
Showing bright red
From the top to the floor.

German, he knew,
Geometry, too.
So gentle and wise
With a high I.Q.

Gentle and kind
A genius, no doubt,
He'd help anyone,
That's what he's about!

Geometry

Germ
La

My Night Light

It's time for bed,
My light shines bright,

I like to see
It light the night,

And in my bed,
I feel all right,

I'm all tucked in
'neath blankets tight,

And soon I'll dream,
I'll take delight,

For I will soar
In dreams of flight,

Above the clouds
And rainbow bright,

Above the clouds,
I'll breath a sigh.

Spring

The welcome spring
Is a beautiful thing,

Birds on the wing
All start to sing.

Warm breezes blowing
And daffodils glowing!

Pink Ink

If I had
Some pink ink,

I'd take it to
The skating rink!

I'd paint the ice
With pink ink,

And ask the world,
"What do you think?"

The Bird

The first bird of spring

Was chirping his song.

He dug in the dirt,

It didn't take too long . . .

He pulled out a worm!

A girl watched, you see.

The bird chirped some more,

Atop a fir tree.

K and N

A K and an N
Make a funny pair,
When they get together
We stop and stare!

For K becomes silent
When next to N's face.
It's not a k-not
But a knot in my lace.

My shoelace is knotted,
But not with a k-not,
I'd better untie it
And straighten a lot.

I'll knock on the door
When the knot is gone,
I'll knock for my friend,
I'll knock until dawn!

My friend doesn't hear,
I knocked with my knees!
My knees hurt from knocking,
I wish I had keys!

I know I should go,
It's lunchtime, I think,
I'll cut up some fruit
With the knife near the sink,

And think of the knot
And my knocking day,
And 'bout K and N
And the silent K.

Silly Goat

Silly goat
Sits in a boat.

Silly goat's
Boat floats.

Silly goat
Is eating oats,

Wearing a coat
In a boat.

Eating oats!
Silly goat!

Stop That Noise!

Stop that racket,
Stop that noise!
Time to pick up
All these toys!

Mom is angry,
Tempers boil,
She is wound up
Like a coil!

Pick up toys,
Sweep up soil,
Get those coins
And wipe that oil!

Pick up paper
And bits of foil,
Time to hurry,
Time to toil!

When we've finished
We rejoice,
Mom has found
Her quiet voice!

City Sounds, Country Sounds

In the city,
Cars all "HONK!"
In the city,
Subways "BONK!"
And "CLONK!"
As coins drop,
In the city.

In the country,
Geese all "HONK!"
In the country,
Pinecones "BONK!"
And "CLONK!"
As they fall,
In the country.

oo

The Zoo

We went to the zoo,
And saw a kangaroo!
When her joey came out,
I said, "Boo!"

We went to the zoo,
And saw an owl, too!
When he flew past me,
I heard him say, "Whoo!"

I like it at the zoo,
But I didn't hear a "Moo!"
And now I want to know,
Do you like it, too?

Cookies

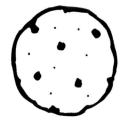

I like cookies and
A really good book.

I like to read
Beside a bubbly brook.

I like to bake
And I like to cook.

Now I'm eating cookies
Beside the bubbly brook!

The Apple Core

I ate an apple,
All but the core,

Wanting to have more,
I went to the store.

My feet were hurting,
It really was a chore.

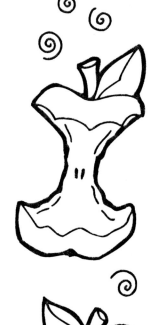

When I got back,
I saw I had a sore

Right on my foot,
Where my shoe wore!

Feeling really down,
Sad and sore and poor,

I ate an apple,
Right to the core!

Our Mouse

A mouse was in our house,
Oh no, oh me, oh my!
Soft and round was he.
He wasn't very shy!

He ran into the kitchen,
Around, around, around!
Did he scout for food?
He covered lots of ground!

We will never know,
He did not stop to say.
The cat found him today,
Our mouse has run away!

Mr. Brown

Dear old Mr. Brown,
His hat down to his brow,
Walked five miles to town,
And saw a friendly cow.

He chatted with the cow,
The cow who lived near town,
The cow who spoke somehow,
And they walked into town.

A Boy and His Toy

A boy was sick in bed,
And so his mother brought,
A toy to give the boy,
A toy that she just bought.

A cowboy was the toy,
A cowboy and his horse.
The boy was filled with joy,
He played with them, of course.

And when the boy was well,
Outside he took his toys,
And played with them out there,
Joined by other boys.

Phil, the Photographer

Phil is a photographer
And such a curious man,
He phones me 'bout the elephants
On any day he can.

He photographs the elephants,
The big ones and the small,
And once he climbed up in a tree
To photograph them all!

Shhh . . .

Shhh . . . Baby Shelley sleeps,

Shhh . . . she sleeps in a shell,

Shhh . . . shining stars will show

Shhh . . . sheep shall sing

Shhh . . . ships slip and slap

Shhh . . . Shelley sleeps in shade.

SH

I Wish

I wish that I
Could catch a fish,
I'd eat him from
A shiny dish.

I wish that I
Could dash in a flash,
I'd come in first
And break the sash!

This and That

"This" is very tall,
"That" is very small,
"This" is in the yard,
"That" is in the hall.

"This" runs really fast,
"That" runs really slow,
"This" is very high,
"That" is very low.

When they meet a friend,
They say, "How do you do?"
I think that you would like them,
And they would like you, too.

Mother Nature

No one can paint a picture

Like Mother Nature can.

No one else can capture

The colors of the land.

No one can paint the creatures

Like Mother Nature can,

Showing all the features

That make them fierce and grand.

No one can make a sculpture

Like Mother Nature can,

From red rock shapes and spires

To clouds shaped by her hand.

Blue

I like blue.

My favorite color is blue.

Why? I don't have a clue.

But it's true, I like blue.

I Swung in a Swing

I swung in a swing
As high as can be.

I hung in the air
So light and free.

All of a sudden
A bee clung to me!

Before I could stop him,
That bee stung me!

The Skunk

As I was resting,
Upon the top bunk,
I looked out the window,
And saw a fat skunk!

That skunk stunk!

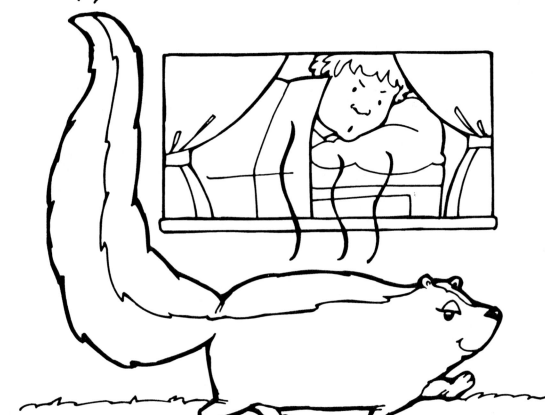

WH Questions

"Where are you going?"
"Who will you see?"

Oh, no, my dad's asking
Questions of me!

"Why are you going?"
"When will you call?"
"What will you do?"

I hope this is all.

Is he just nosy?
Or maybe he cares,
With his "who," "what,"
"Why," and "wheres."

48